SCIENCE SKILLS SORTED

PLANTS

ANGELA ROYSTON

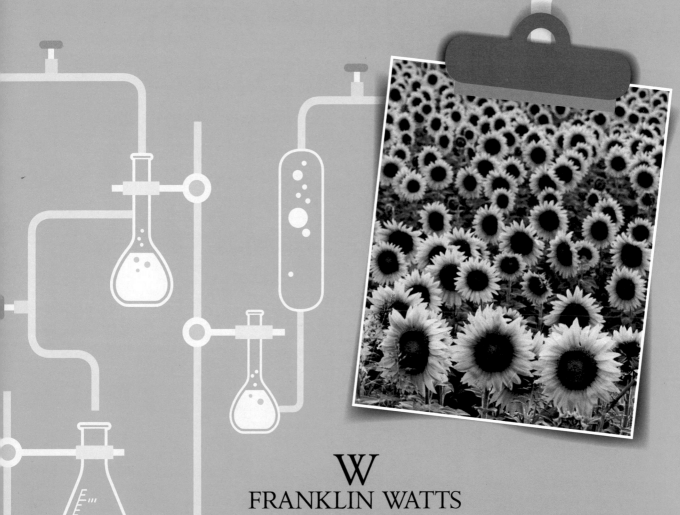

W
FRANKLIN WATTS
LONDON•SYDNEY

Franklin Watts
First published in Great Britain in 2017 by The Watts Publishing Group

Credits
Series Editor: Amy Pimperton
Series Designer: Emma DeBanks
Picture Researcher: Diana Morris
Picture credits: aaabbbccc/Shutterstock: 12t. ajt/Shutterstock: 27cr. Andriano/
Shutterstock: 7bl, 29b. AP/PAI: 20b. Artistas/Shutterstock: 14c. art-partner images/Getty
Images: 21b. Bonnie Taylor Barry/Shutterstock: 22bl. Radu Bercan/Shutterstock: 19c. Billion
Photos/Shutterstock: 15c. Biofoto Associates/SPL: 18c. Gary Blakeley/Shutterstock 17b. ByEmo/
Shutterstock: 11br. Nigel Catlin/FLPA: 8t. Chainfoto24/Shutterstock: 12c. Paul Crash/
Shutterstock: 3bc. Stefan Diller/SPL: 15b. Neil Donoghue/Shutterstock: 11bl. Dreamy Girl/
Shutterstock: 22t. Eye of Science/SPL: 14t. fotomirk/Shutterstock: 27c. Olga Glinskaja/
Shutterstock: 21c. Hhelene/Shutterstock: 9t. Jeremy Sutton-Hibbert/Alamy: 27b. Homey
Design/Shutterstock: 23ca. Jiang Hongyan/Shutterstock: 17t. Bjørn Hovdal/Deamstime: 27t.
iko/Shutterstock: 6t. javarman/Shutterstock: 5b. Kichigin/Shutterstock: 8b. Igor Kovalchuk/
Shutterstock: 25t. R Lan/Shutterstock: 21t. Katrina Leigh/Shutterstock: 9b. Libra/Shutterstock: 19t.
Likar/Shutterstock: 24t. Little_Desire/Shutterstock: 25b. Louisebittersweet/Dreamstime: 18b. tea
maeklong/Shutterstock: 18t. majaan/Shutterstock: 22br. Anna Minsk/Shutterstock: 26b. Miny/
Shutterstock: 23c. msgrafixx/Shutterstock: 10t. Maks Narodenko/Shutterstock: 17c. Njene/
Shutterstock: 3br, 24b. Noppharat4569/Shutterstock: 4t. Oshcan/Getty Images: front cover.
Natalya Osipova/Shutterstock: 26c. pixinoo/Shutterstock: 6b. pogonici/Shutterstock: 16t, 28b.
Valentina Razumova/Shutterstock: 23b. Werner Rebel/Shutterstock: 4b. Peter Roeder/
Dreamstime: 20c. Rssooli/Shutterstock: 14b. Sakarin Sawasdinaka/Shutterstock: 27cl. ScripX/
Shutterstock: 13b. Dipak Shelare/Shutterstock: 11t. Andrei Shumskiy/Shutterstock: 7r, 19b, 29t.
Gary K Smith/FLPA: 26t. Olaf Speier/Shutterstock: 20t. Stockr/Shutterstock: 12b. Navakun
Suwantragul/Shutterstock: 10b, 29c. Syda productions/Shutterstock: 16cl. Irinia Tischenko/
Shutterstock: 25tc. Tim UR/Shutterstock: 23t. vetasster/Shutterstock: 15t. Frank Vicentz/CC Wikimedia: 10c.
Wam1975/Dreamstime: 1. wawritto/Shutterstock: 5t. WHA/Photoshot: 16cr. winnond/Shutterstock: 6c.

HB ISBN 978 1 4451 5093 2
PB ISBN 978 1 4451 5094 9

Printed in China

Franklin Watts
An imprint of
Hachette Children's Group
Part of The Watts Publishing Group
Carmelite House
50 Victoria Embankment
London EC4Y 0DZ

An Hachette UK Company
www.hachette.co.uk

www.franklinwatts.co.uk

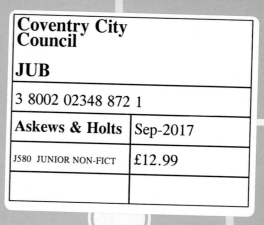

MIX
Paper from
responsible sources
FSC® C104740

CONTENTS

Worlds in **bold** can be found in the glossary on page 30.

WHAT MAKES A PLANT A PLANT?

Plants are living things that have roots, a trunk or stem, leaves, and the ability to produce seeds that will grow into new plants.

Plants include trees and bushes, which have wooden trunks and branches. Other plants are **vines**, wild flowers, grasses, ferns and mosses.

Conifer trees, such as pine, have needles instead of broad leaves and they produce new seeds in cones. Many other plants have flowers, in which new seeds develop, while ferns and mosses grow from **spores** not seeds.

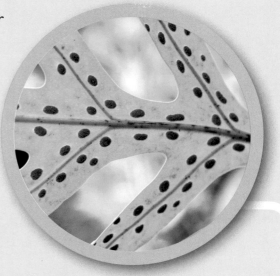

Brown clusters of spores form under the fronds of a fern.

POLLINATION

A flower produces a new seed when one of its female eggs, or **ovules**, combines with a grain of male **pollen** from another flower of the same type. This is called pollination. Colourful flowers rely on insects – particularly bees – or birds to carry the pollen from flower to flower.

Grasses and many trees have small green flowers, whose pollen is blown through the air by the wind. Spores are also spread by the wind.

pollen

Grasses produce many small flowers at the top of tall stems. The wind blows clouds of pollen from the flowers.

PHOTOSYNTHESIS

The most important feature that plants share is their ability to make food. The process is called **photosynthesis** and it mostly takes place in the leaves. Water, taken in through the roots, is combined with **carbon dioxide** from the air to make sugar.

This **chemical reaction** could not happen without **chlorophyll**, a green substance contained in the leaves. Chlorophyll takes in energy from light and then releases the energy to power the chemical reaction. The sugar travels from the leaves along thin **veins** to feed every part of the plant.

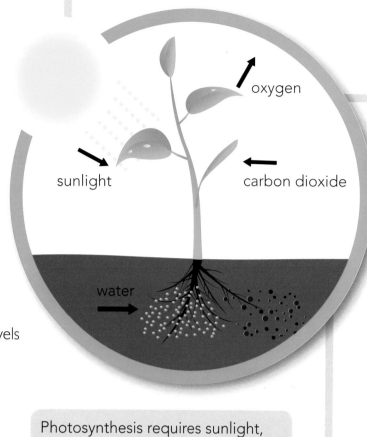

oxygen

sunlight

carbon dioxide

water

Photosynthesis requires sunlight, the gas carbon dioxide and water.

VITAL PLANTS

Animals, including humans, could not survive without plants. Some animals feed directly on plants, others feed on these plant-eating animals. However, if you trace what each animal in a **food chain** eats, the chain always begins with plants. Plants also keep the air we breathe stocked with **oxygen**. Photosynthesis produces oxygen as a waste gas, which is released into the air. Animals use oxygen to change food into energy, and cannot survive without it.

A cheetah is a meat-eater that hunts wildebeest and other animals. Wildebeest feed on grass and other plant leaves.

THE SCIENCE OF PLANTS

Plants are incredibly useful to scientists. Plants contain chemicals and materials that scientists explore and test to see how they can be used.

Many everyday products, from toothpaste to T-shirts, contain ingredients that come from plants. New plants are being discovered all the time and some have unique properties, such as the ability to cure particular diseases.

Fluffy cotton **bolls** protect the cotton plant seeds inside. Bolls are turned into cotton fibres to make clothing.

Medicines made from the Madagascar periwinkle are used to treat cancer.

PERFECT PLANTS

Plants are perfect subjects to investigate. Unlike animals, they cannot run away and they do not feel pain. It is easy to grow the large numbers of plants that scientists need to conduct experiments and to check that the same **outcome** always occurs. Often experiments are repeated with small changes to see how the change affects the outcome.

You can experiment with plants too. This book includes experiments that test what plants need to grow, and whether plants prefer one kind of liquid or colour of light to another. You can explore why leaves change colour in the autumn and you can even **clone** some plants.

Modern farming allows thousands of plants to be grown in nurseries.

WORKING SCIENTIFICALLY

In this book, you'll find a range of experiments or investigations that will help you discover how plants work.

To do experiments, scientists use careful, logical methods to make sure they get reliable results. The experiments in this book use four key scientific methods, along with an easy acronym to help you remember them: **ATOM**.

 ## ASK

What do you want to find out?

Asking questions is a really important part of science. Scientists think about what questions they want to answer, and how to do that.

 ## TEST

Setting up an experiment that will test ideas and answer questions

Scientists then design experiments to answer their questions. A test works best if you only test for one thing at a time.

 ## OBSERVE

Key things to look out for

Scientists watch their experiments closely to see what is happening.

 ## MEASURE

Measuring and recording results, such as temperatures, sizes or amounts of time

Making accurate measurements and recording the results shows what the experiment has revealed.

WHAT NEXT?

After each experiment, the 'What next?' section gives you ideas for more activities and experiments or ways to display your results.

SEEDS

A seed contains a store of food and an undeveloped plant, called an **embryo**. When the seed takes in water, it swells and the embryo begins to grow. It uses the food stored in the seed while its roots grow down into the soil. This is called germination.

As it takes in water from the soil through its root, the shoot grows up through the soil into the light. When the shoot's first two leaves open, they can begin to photosynthesise (see p. 5).

This bean has been cut in half to show how a new plant begins to grow.

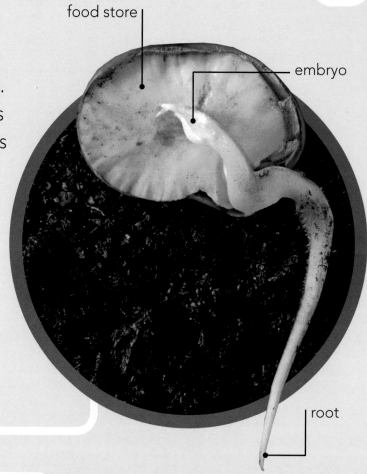

food store

embryo

root

SPEEDY AND SLOW

Some plants grow from seeds faster than others. The seeds of **weeds** and wild flowers, such as dandelions and chickweed, grow almost at once. Some desert flowers lie **dormant** as seeds in the ground and wait for months or years for a heavy shower of rain. Then the seeds grow quickly into plants with flowers, and make new seeds before the ground dries up again.

The seeds of wild flowers, such as these daisies, take root and grow quickly on a patch of wasteland.

SCIENCE EXPERIMENT:

THE SEED RACE

Plant different types of seed to find out which germinates first and which grows fastest.

runner bean seeds

 ASK

Which type of seed will grow the fastest? Which will be the first to sprout?

 TEST

- Fill each tray with compost so it is about 3 cm deep.
- Add water to make the compost damp.
- Label one tray 'peas'. Plant each pea seed 5 cm apart, just below the surface.
- Label and plant the runner beans and cress seeds in the other two trays.
- Place the trays in a warm, dark place.

 OBSERVE

When the first seeds in a tray sprout, place the tray near a well-lit window. Check all the trays every day. Add water to keep the compost damp.

 MEASURE

Every four days, measure the height of the tallest seedling in each tray. Draw a graph for each type of seed. Which seed grew fastest and so won the race?

WHAT NEXT?

About three weeks after they sprout, carefully scoop the seedlings from their trays and plant them in small plant pots filled with extra compost so they can continue to grow. Once the plants are big enough, plant them in a vegetable patch in your garden or at school.

A seedling unfurls its first two leaves and grows more roots in the first few days after germination.

PLANT DEFENCE

Many plants have developed different ways of protecting themselves from being eaten. Some plants have sharp thorns or spiky leaves, while others contain **toxins** that are harmful if eaten. A few plants combine spikes with poisonous **acids**.

A nettle is covered with tiny hair-like stingers, which contain **formic acid**. When you touch a hair, the tip of the stinger breaks off and the acid shoots into your skin, causing an itchy, painful rash.

A nettle's tiny stingers contain poison, which protects the plant from being eaten or attacked by animals.

WHAT IS AN ACID?

Acids are chemicals that are **corrosive** and **neutralise alkalis**. Alkalis are chemicals that are also corrosive and neutralise acids. Scientists test for acids and alkalis using universal indicator paper and a scale, which gives a **pH value** between 0 and 14. Acids turn the paper red, orange or yellow and measure between 0 and 7, with 0 being the most acidic. Alkalis turn the paper green, blue or purple and measure between 7 and 14.

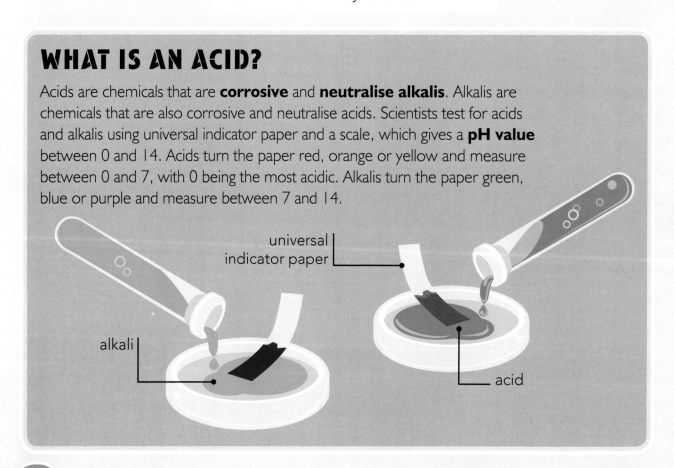

universal indicator paper

alkali

acid

YOU WILL NEED:

5 plastic cups
Labels
Gloves
Freshly picked nettles
Lemon juice, milk, vinegar, window cleaner
Measuring jug
5 teaspoons
Universal indicator paper
Kitchen towel

ACID TEST

Many foods and everyday products are acidic. How does the acid in a nettle compare with them?

Ask an adult to supervise you when using glass cleaner or other household products.

Wash your hands after you have done this experiment.

 ASK

Is a nettle more or less acidic than the other four everyday substances you will test?

 TEST

- Label each cup with one of the substances.
- Wearing gloves, crush four or five nettle leaves in the 'nettle' cup with a teaspoon.
- Pour 50 ml of water into each plastic cup.
- Using a clean spoon each time, mix a teaspoon of each liquid you are testing into its plastic cup.
- Dip a strip of univeral indicator paper into the first cup and leave for 20 seconds. Remove the paper and place it on a clean piece of kitchen towel.
- Repeat the last step with each remaining cup in turn.

 OBSERVE

Note how quickly the universal indicator paper changes colour. Which strip is the reddest?

 MEASURE

Use this universal indicator chart to match the colour of each strip to its pH value. Draw a bar chart to show how the nettle compares with the other liquids.

Universal indicator chart

Acid   Alkali

0   7   14

pH Value

Products that contain strong acids or alkalis usually carry a warning sign to show that they are dangerous and should be handled carefully.

WHAT NEXT?

Test some more household items to work out their acid or alkali pH values, such as toothpaste, washing up liquid and tap water.

WHAT PLANTS NEED TO GROW

Plants need the right conditions to grow well. These conditions include temperature, the type of soil and how much light they receive. Some plants need to be in a sunny place, others, such as rainforest plants, prefer a shady place.

Poppies grow well in bright sunshine.

WATER

Most of all plants need water. Most plants rely on rainwater to keep their soils moist. **Tropical** rainforest plants get rain almost every day.

Rainforest plants get so much rain they grow very close together. Some grow very tall.

FERTILISERS

Soil contains nutrients, such as **nitrogen**, **phosphorus** and **potassium**. Plants use these chemicals from the soil to photosynthesise, breathe and grow. **Fertilisers** contain extra nutrients, so farmers add them to the soil to help their crops grow even better.

This farmer is spraying fertiliser onto the soil so that his plants will produce a bigger crop.

SCIENCE EXPERIMENT:

ADDED EXTRAS

The liquids we drink are mostly made up of water that contains other things. Fruit juice and cola contain sugar, and milk contains fats and proteins. Will plants grow better when they are 'watered' with our drinks?

Ask

Which liquid will most help a plant to grow?

Test

- Measure 100 ml of water and pour it into the bowl of one of the plants.
- Repeat with the other liquids and plants.
- Label each bowl with its liquid.
- Place the bowls and pots on a sunny windowsill.

Observe

Check the plants every few hours to see which plant begins to flop first. Look closely at the leaves and stem. Keep checking for a few days and record what happens to each plant.

Measure

Measure the height of each plant every day. Draw a graph to show how each plant grew. Did you predict correctly?

When plants don't have enough to 'drink' the stems droop and the leaves shrivel up as the plant dries out.

WHAT NEXT?

Use the drinks' packaging to check the amount of sugar in each liquid. Check the pH level of each liquid (see pp. 10–11). Does this help you explain the outcome?

SURVIVING A DROUGHT

Plants take in water through tiny hairs on their roots. The water moves through the roots into narrow tubes, called **xylem**, in the stem. From the stem, water travels to every leaf, bud, flower or fruit. You can see some xylem if you examine a stalk of celery. The tubes end in stringy bits at the bottom of the stalk.

The dark green dots on this thin slice of celery stem are the plant's xylem.

WATER IN FLOWERS

When a flower has finished its job of fertilising seeds, it wilts. The plant cuts the water supply to the flowers and the petals crumple, shrink and fall off. The fruits and seeds can then take in more water and begin to swell and ripen.

Pea plants produce pods of seeds (peas). The pod protects the seeds as they swell and ripen.

SHORT OF WATER

You can see how important water is to a plant by watching what happens when it is short of water. The plant loses its rigidity – the flowers and leaves droop, dry up and fall off. In some plants the whole stem droops too. In extreme cases, the plant may die.

These crops are wilting because there is a drought – a period when there is little or no rain over a long period of time.

 SCIENCE EXPERIMENT:

THIRSTY PLANTS

Some plants can survive without water better than others. Test different plants and compare what happens as they dry up and then are watered again.

YOU WILL NEED:

4 small bunches of herbs, such as basil, mint, parsley and rosemary
Water and a measuring jug
4 plastic tumblers
Notebook and pen

Ask

Which plant will survive longest without water?

Test

- Place each herb in an empty tumbler and wait until it wilts. (Some may wilt quickly, so check the plants two or three times each day.)
- When each herb wilts, pour 100 ml of water into its tumbler.

Rosemary   Mint   Parsley   Basil

Observe

Note how long each herb lasts before it wilts. What happens when you water it again?

Measure

Record whether each herb recovers when you water it, and how long it takes. Draw bar charts to compare how well the herbs lasted without water and how quickly they recovered.

WHAT NEXT?

Compare the stems of each herb to see whether there is a link between the rigidity or bendiness of the stem and the results. Repeat the experiment with plants that have flowers, such as a rose. Do you get the same result?

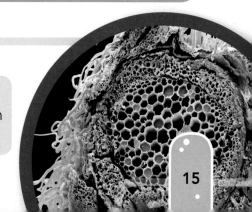

This picture shows a close up of the xylem in a rosemary stem.

15

WATER CONTENT

Water content is the amount of water something contains. The water content of fruit and vegetables is between 80 and 95 per cent. A quick way to check water content is to test whether something sinks or floats in water. The faster it sinks, the less water it contains.

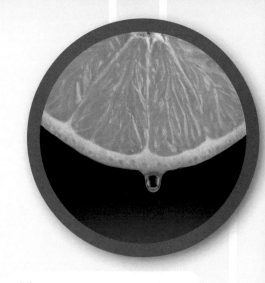

Most oranges contain about 70 ml of juice.

A pepper floats because it is filled with air, which is lighter than water.

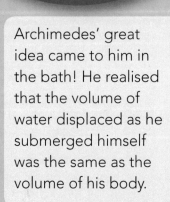

DENSITY

Density is a more accurate way to measure water content. The density of water is one gramme per **cubic centimetre** (1 g/cc). An object that floats is less dense or has the same density as water. An object that sinks is denser than water.

Density is calculated by dividing the weight of an object by its volume, but how do you measure the volume of fruit and vegetables that have irregular shapes? An ancient Greek scientist called Archimedes solved the problem. He sank the object in a container filled with water and measured the volume of water that spilled over.

Archimedes' great idea came to him in the bath! He realised that the volume of water displaced as he submerged himself was the same as the volume of his body.

SCIENCE EXPERIMENT:

SINK OR FLOAT?

You can use Archimedes' method to calculate whether various fruits and vegetables are more or less dense than water and to calculate their volume.

 ## Ask

Which items will float? Will any sink? Which one do you predict has the lowest water content?

 ## Test

- Weigh each fruit or vegetable and note its weight.
- Pour water into the jug up to the 600 cc mark.
- Carefully place the tomato in the water.
- If it floats, push it below the surface with the straw.
- Read the water level on the jug and note it down.
- Repeat with the other items.

 ## Observe

Which fruits and vegetables float and which sink? Were your predictions correct?

 ## Measure

Use the two readings of water level in the jug to calculate the volume of each fruit or vegetable. Divide the weight of each by its volume to get the density. The fruit or vegetable with the highest density has the lowest water content.

WHAT NEXT?

Repeat the experiment using an orange, a banana, an apple and a parsnip. See if you can find out why heavy, metal ships are able to float on water without sinking to the bottom of the ocean?

a huge
container ship

HOW LEAVES WORK

Leaves are food factories – they manufacture a sugary, liquid sap, which feeds the whole plant. Only green plants can make their own food and their leaves are brilliantly structured to photosynthesise sugar from carbon dioxide and water.

The lines on a leaf are called veins. They consist of bundles of tubes that bring water into the leaf and carry away the sugary sap.

stomata

STRUCTURE OF A LEAF

Tiny **pores** (holes) in the leaf, called **stomata**, open to let carbon dioxide from the air into the leaf and oxygen gas out. The leaf sucks up water through the roots and xylem. Green chlorophyll absorbs energy from sunlight and this drives the reaction that turns carbon dioxide and water into sugar. The surface of the leaf is protected by a tough, transparent layer, which allows sunlight through.

LEAVES LOVE SUNLIGHT!

Leaves are flat and thin to give a large area for sunlight to strike. A plant moves its leaves so that the flat surface faces the Sun. As the Sun moves across the sky, the leaves turn to follow the Sun.

Sunflowers slowly turn to face the Sun and soak up as much sunlight as they can.

BLOCKING OUT THE LIGHT

Explore what happens to a leaf when light cannot reach all or part of a leaf.

 ASK

What happens to the chlorophyll in a leaf when it is deprived of light?

 TEST

• Use the colour chart to note each plant's leaf colour.
• Cut the sticky paper into different sizes and shapes, and make some that cover a whole leaf of each plant.
• Stick the shapes to some of the leaves of each plant. Stick some on top of the leaf; stick some underneath.
• Carefully remove the shapes after a week.

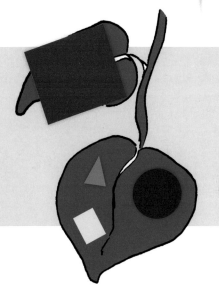

 OBSERVE

What has happened to the patches of leaf below the shapes? Did it make a difference if the shape was on top of, or underneath, the leaf?

WHAT NEXT?

Record how long it takes for each leaf to return to its original colour.

 MEASURE

Match the colour of the patches to the colours on the charts. Count the number of patches for each colour. Are the colours different for each plant?

HELPING NATURE?

Plants grow best in the summer, when the weather is warm and the days are long and bright. In winter the weather is colder, the days are shorter and the light is dimmer. How can farmers change a crop's environment so that the crop produces a bigger, better harvest?

These farm crops are growing under and through long sheets of polythene.

WARM AND BRIGHT

Some farmers cover vegetable crops with huge polythene sheets, which trap heat and protect the crops from frost. Growing plants indoors or in greenhouses can be expensive, but it allows farmers to give plants extra light as well as heat. Using **artificial** light means that plants can photosynthesise and grow, even when it is dark outside.

Plants grow fast in this special farm building, lit day and night by pink lights.

SCIENCE EXPERIMENT:
TESTING COLOURS

Sunlight looks white, but actually contains all the colours of the rainbow. Do plants use all of the colours it contains? This experiment tests whether some colours help plants grow better than others.

YOU WILL NEED:

4 plants of the same type in separate pots
3 rolls of coloured cellophane
1 roll of clear cellophane
4 sticks about 30 cm long
Scissors
Sticky tape

Ask

Which colour or colours of light will help a plant grow most?

Observe

Check the plants every day. Do you notice any changes?

Measure

Measure the height of each plant at the beginning of the experiment, and then measure the height again after a week. Draw a bar chart to compare the heights for each colour.

Test

- Cut 50 x 50 cm squares of each colour of cellophane.
- Mark the centre of each square by folding into quarters. Cut a small hole at the centre.
- Push a stick into the soil in each plant pot.
- Slide a square of cellophane over each stick until the plant is covered. Tape the cellophane to the stick and tuck in the sides to keep ordinary light out.
- Put the plant pots in a brightly lit place, such as a windowsill.

cellophane

WHAT NEXT?

Remove the cellophane. How long does it take for any or all of the plants to recover?

A glass **prism** can be used to show how white light splits into all of the colours of the rainbow.

FLOWERS AND SEEDS

An ovule becomes a **fertilised** seed when a grain of pollen from another flower combines with it. The male parts of a flower produce pollen, while the female parts receive pollen and pass it to the ovules.

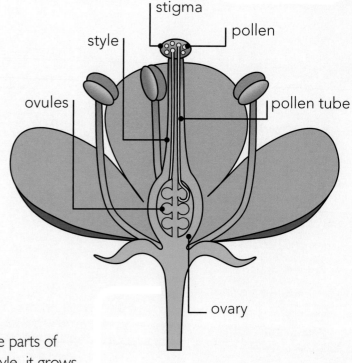

POLLEN TO SEED

The stigma, style, ovary and ovules are the female parts of the flower. When a ripe pollen grain lands on a style, it grows a narrow tube down the style to an ovule below. The pollen then moves down the tube and joins with the ovule. The ovule develops into a seed as the ovary swells into a fruit.

Each grain of pollen grows a tube to reach an ovule in the ovary.

Birds help to scatter the seeds inside these juicy berry fruits.

sycamore seed

SEEDS

Seeds develop better when they fall onto soil some distance from the plant. Many plants, such as sycamore trees, rely on the wind to distribute their seeds. Peas develop in pods that split and catapult their seeds out. Other plants wrap their seeds in juicy fruits. Animals eat the fruits and then drop the seeds or deposit them in their droppings, often far away.

YOU WILL NEED:

2 strawberry plants (Alpine strawberries grow well in a window box)
A window box
Several small, soft paintbrushes
Labels and pen

SCIENCE EXPERIMENT:

GROWING STRAWBERRIES

You can observe how pollination works and a flower produces a fruit and seeds by growing strawberries in pots or in a window box.

 ASK

Which plant will produce the most strawberries?

 TEST

- Plant the strawberry plants in a window box and place it outside or on a window sill.
- Label the plants A and B and water them to keep the soil moist.
- When the plants flower, use a paintbrush to gently move pollen from the flowers of plant A to the flowers of plant B (but be careful not to move pollen from plant B to plant A). Use a different brush for each flower.
- Pick the strawberries as they become ripe.

 OBSERVE

Watch the plants grow. Record the date when the experiment started, when the flowers bud, when they open and when they wilt. Does one plant produce more or fewer strawberries? Why do you think this might be?

 MEASURE

Make a table to record how long it takes for the strawberries to swell and ripen and to show how many strawberries each plant produces.

WHAT NEXT?

Look for the seeds on each strawberry. Most plants hide their seeds inside the fruit, but strawberries embed their seeds on the outside.

strawberry seeds —

AUTUMN COLOURS

In autumn, maple leaves change colour from green to orange to bright red, before they fall from the tree.

Colourful autumn leaves show that winter is coming! Evergreen leaves have a tough, waxy surface to protect them from freezing. Broad, flat leaves, however, would be damaged by frost and so the tree discards them.

WHAT CAUSES THE COLOURS?

Green leaves get their colour from chlorophyll, the chemical needed for photosynthesis (see p. 5). As autumn nights get colder, the leaves stop producing chlorophyll and the green fades, revealing shades of red, orange and yellow. These colours were there all along, but only become visible in the autumn.

Different chemicals in the leaves produce the different colours.

YOU WILL NEED:

Soft leaves from 2 broad-leafed
trees, e.g. maple and lime
Surgical spirit or
rubbing alcohol
Coffee filter paper and scissors
Ruler
2 cups or plastic tumblers
2 pens
Sticky tape

SCIENCE EXPERIMENT:

HIDDEN COLOURS

You don't have to wait until autumn to see the hidden colours in a green leaf. Try this experiment in late summer to reveal the colours below the chlorophyll.

Ask an adult to pour out the surgical spirit or rubbing alcohol and to supervise you while you use them. Never use them by yourself or put them in your mouth as they are highly dangerous.

Ask

Which leaf will reveal the brightest colours?

Test

- Cut the maple leaves into tiny pieces and quarter-fill one of the cups or plastic tumblers.
- Repeat with the lime leaves. Label each tumbler with the name of its leaf.
- Ask an adult to pour in surgical spirit or rubbing alcohol to just cover the leaves, stir and leave to soak for about 30 minutes.
- Cut two 2 cm x 10 cm strips from the coffee filter paper.
- Place a pen across each tumbler and stick a strip of filter paper to it so that the end of the strip just touches the liquid.
- When the liquid reaches the top of the strips, remove and leave to dry.

lime leaf

Lime
Maple

Observe

Watch the liquid from the leaf mixture soak up the strip. Look for the colours that appear on the strip.

Measure

When the strips are dry, measure the width of each band of colour. Stick the strips to a larger piece of paper to display the results.

WHAT NEXT?

Repeat with different leaves, including a broad evergreen leaf, such as ivy.

ivy leaf

CLONING PLANTS

Cloning is a way of producing new plants from a part of an existing plant. The new plants are then identical to the original plant, unlike plants grown from seeds, which grow into uniquely different plants.

runner

NATURAL CLONING

Some plants, such as strawberries, can clone themselves. Strawberries produce stems, called runners, which grow along the ground before putting down roots. Plants that grow from bulbs often clone themselves too. The bulbs split into two or more bulbs, which then grow into separate plants.

A strawberry plant grows a runner that a new plant then grows from.

TAKING CUTTINGS

The easiest way to clone some plants is to take a **cutting** by snipping off a section of stem with leaves and putting it in water. After a while the stem produces new roots and can be planted into soil.

cutting

roots

Geranium plants are easy to grow from cuttings.

WHAT CAN YOU CLONE?

You can clone a plant from its stem, its roots or a bulb, but some plants are easier to clone than others. Can you clone plants from pieces of vegetable?

YOU WiLL NEED:

A tray or shallow bowl
Water
Kitchen towel
A carrot, a garlic clove,
a leek and a lettuce
Notepad and pen
Camera

ASK

Which vegetable will grow into a whole new plant?

clove of garlic _____

TEST

- Cut off the flat end of the carrot.
- Cut off the bottom of the leek and the bottom of the lettuce.
- Place two sheets of kitchen towel in the tray and cover with enough water to soak the paper.
- Put the vegetables and the clove of garlic on top of the kitchen roll.

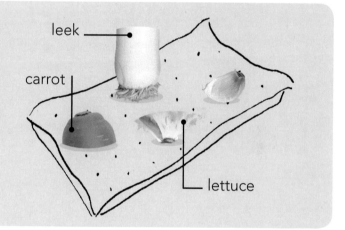

leek

carrot

lettuce

OBSERVE

Check the tray every day and add water to keep the paper moist. Look for the appearance of tiny roots or shoots. Take a photograph every other day.

WHAT NEXT?

If any of your vegetables produce roots and shoots, plant them in a plant pot filled with compost and you may be able to grow a cloned plant. *

One of the most famous cloning experiments was the cloning of Dolly the Sheep. Scientists cloned her in 1995 from a single **cell**!

MEASURE

After a week, measure any roots or shoots that have grown. Which clone is most successful? Use your photos to make a display.

* see note on page 32.

READING YOUR RESULTS

When scientists do experiments, they get results. Even if nothing happened as they expected, that is a result too! All results can be useful, but it is important to understand them. Here are some guidelines that scientists use to learn from their results.

USE A CONTROL

In the Added Extras experiment (p. 13), the 'control' is the plant that you give the water to. A control is a normal version of the set-up, without the things that are being tested – in this case the milk, orange juice and cola.

It's really important that apart from the thing being tested, the control version matches the test version in every way. So you use the same type of plant, size of pot, and amount of soil and liquid as the other plants. Then you know that any differences in your results are purely down to the liquids.

REPEAT AND VERIFY

An experiment may work well once, but what if that was a fluke? So that they can be sure of their results, scientists often repeat an experiment several times to verify their results.

CHECK FOR BIAS

If you're *really* hoping for an exciting result, it's possible you might accidentally-on-purpose 'help' your experiment along by ignoring something that doesn't fit with what you wanted. This is called 'bias' and can happen without you even realising it.

OUTLIERS

What if you were conducting the Acid Test experiment (p. 11) and the milk sample registered as more acidic than the vinegar?

You'd probably be quite surprised, because if you had acid indigestion, you would be more likely to drink milk to settle your stomach than vinegar! This unusual result is called an outlier and scientists have to check outliers carefully and work out why they have happened. For example, the milk might have gone sour, which increases its acidity.

KEEPING RECORDS

Writing down the details of each experiment and what the results were is essential for scientists. Not only does it help explain their work to others; it also means they can use results to look for patterns. For example, in the Hidden Colours experiment (p. 25), is there a link between the colours produced and the colours of the leaves in autumn?

MAKING MISTAKES

If you spot a mistake, start the experiment again. It would be an even bigger mistake to use the results from a badly run experiment.

However, if a mistake makes something interesting happen, you could set up a new experiment to test for that instead. Many important discoveries have been made this way. For example, artificial sweeteners were discovered by a chemist who forgot to wash his hands after handling coal and other chemicals. When he got home he noticed his hands tasted sweet!

GLOSSARY

acid A substance that turns universal indicator paper red. Very strong acids can dissolve some metals.

alkali A substance that turns universal indicator paper blue and neutralises acids.

artificial Not occurring naturally; man-made.

boll A type of round seed pod.

carbon dioxide One of the mixture of gases that make up the Earth's atmosphere.

cell The smallest structure in the body of a living thing; cells contain a nucleus.

chemical reaction When two or more chemicals combine to form a substance.

chlorophyll The green substance in plants that absorbs energy from light.

clone An identical copy.

corrosive Able to eat away or break up a substance.

cubic centimetre (cc) A cube that measures 1 cm high x 1 cm wide x 1 cm deep.

cutting Part of the stem or root of a plant, which can be used to grow an identical plant.

density The weight of an object, or its mass, compared to its volume.

dormant A plant that is alive, but not growing at that time.

embryo A tiny part inside a seed that grows into a new plant.

fertilised A seed that is able to grow, as male pollen has joined with a female ovule.

fertiliser A chemical or natural substance that is added to soil to help plants grow.

food chain A sequence of living things in which one eats the next, which eats the next, and so on.

formic acid An acid that is found in the stings of nettles, some other plants and in the stings of some ants.

neutralise To cancel out. An alkali neutralises an acid in the same way that cold water neutralises hot water.

nitrogen A chemical that can be used as a nutrient to help plants and living things to grow.

outcome A result.

ovule A female egg inside a plant before it is fertilised.

oxygen A gas that most living things, including humans, need to take in to survive.

pH value A reading on a scale that shows how acidic or alkali something is.

phosphorus A chemical that plants use to help them grow.

photosynthesis The chemical reaction in plants that turns carbon dioxide, light and water into the sugars that a plant feeds on.

pollen Fine, yellow dust grains that fertilise ovules.

pore A tiny hole in a leaf or in human skin that gases and liquids can pass through.

potassium A chemical that plants use to help them grow.

prism A 3D geometric glass object with a triangular shape, used to split white light into the colour rays of the spectrum.

spore A tiny body which, if the conditions are right, can develop into a new individual. Ferns, mosses, fungi and bacteria all reproduce using spores.

stomata The tiny holes in a leaf through which carbon dioxide enters the leaf and oxygen leaves it.

toxin Poison produced by a plant or animal.

tropical Something that lives in the tropics, the hot, wet areas of the Earth above and below the Equator.

veins Tiny tubes that carry sugar and water in a leaf.

vine A plant with a long, woody stem that clings to and climbs up walls or trees.

weeds Wild flowers that grow in the wrong place, such as gardens, where they were not deliberately planted.

xylem Tiny, tough tubes in a plant stem that carry water and nutrients from the soil and help to support the plant.

BOOKS

All About Biology by Robert Winston (Dorling Kindersley)

Amazing Science: Plants by Sally Hewitt (Wayland)

Cycles in Nature: Plant Life by Theresa Greenaway (Wayland)

Moving Up with Science: Plants by Peter Riley (Franklin Watts)

The Big Countdown: 10,000 Poisonous Plants in the World by Paul Rockett (Franklin Watts)

Other books in this series:

Science Skills Sorted: Habitats

Science Skills Sorted: Human and Animal Bodies

Science Skills Sorted: Life Cycles

Science Skills Sorted: Evolution and Classification

Science Skills Sorted: Rocks and Fossils

WEBSITES

www.dkfindout.com/uk/animals-and-nature/plants/how-plants-grow/
This website includes information about how plants grow, the different parts of a plant and a video showing how a runner bean grows.

http://earthsky.org/human-world/artificial-light-plant-growth
Two scientists explain why sunlight is the best light with which to grow plants.

www.education.com/science-fair/botany/
Ten plant experiments for kids to do at home or in school.

www.ducksters.com/science/acids_and_bases.php
A website that explains all about acids and alkalis and the pH value scale.

Every effort has been made by the Publishers to ensure that the websites in this book are suitable for children, that they are of the highest educational value, and that they contain no inappropriate or offensive material. However, because of the nature of the Internet, it is impossible to guarantee that the contents of these sites will not be altered. We strongly advise that Internet access is supervised by a responsible adult.

INDEX

* Your carrot, lettuce and leek may grow shoots and roots, but they will not grow any new vegetables. If your garlic clove grows shoots and roots, try planting it and it may grow a whole new garlic bulb, which you can eat.

SCIENCE SKILLS SORTED
These are the lists of contents for the titles in the Science Skills Sorted series:

PLANTS

What makes a plant a plant? • The science of plants • Working scientifically • Seeds • Plant defence • What plants need to grow • Surviving a drought • Water content • How leaves work • Helping nature • Flowers and seeds • Autumn colours • Cloning plants • Reading your results • Glossary and further information • Index

HABITATS

What is a habitat? • The science of habitats • Working scientifically • Wildlife habitats • Adaptations • Moving in • Blending in • Extreme habitats • Keystone species • How trees help • Balancing the numbers • Building the environment • Climate change • Reading your results • Glossary and further information • Index

LIFE CYCLES

What is a life cycle? • The science of life cycles • Working scientifically • From seed to seed • Eggs and babies • Metamorphosis • Finding a mate • Dividing bacteria • Budding yeast • Spreading out • Generations • Life cycle maths • Hitching a ride • Reading your results • Glossary and further information • Index

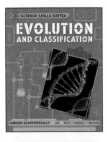

EVOLUTION AND CLASSIFICATION

What is evolution? • The science of evolution • Working scientifically • Evolution in action • Survival of the fittest • Finding food • Adapting to habitats • Winning a mate • Genes and generations • Classification • Sorting it out • Living relatives • The DNA key • Reading your results • Glossary and further information • Index

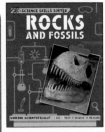

ROCKS AND FOSSILS

What are rocks, minerals and fossils? • The science of rocks and fossils • Working scientifically • Types of rock • Rocks and water • Minerals and crystals • How hard? • Weathering and erosion • Expanding ice • Making mountains • Volcanoes and earthquakes • How fossils form • Fossil puzzles • Reading your results • Glossary and further information • Index

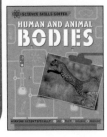

HUMAN AND ANIMAL BODIES

Humans and other animals? • Studying humans and animals • Working scientifically • Bones • Moving on land • Built to fly • Super streamlined • Sharp sight • Locating sound • Interesting smell • Teeth and beaks • Breathing • Unique individuals • Reading your results • Glossary and further information • Index